DO IT

AGAIN,

LORD!

30 DAYS OF HOPE-FILLED PRAYER FOR REVIVAL

Compiled and Edited by CAROL MADISON

A *Prayer*CONNECT Book

PRAYERSHOP
PUBLISHING

Terre Haute, Indiana

PrayerShop Publishing is the publishing arm of the Church Prayer Leaders Network. The Church Prayer Leaders Network exists to equip and inspire local churches and their prayer leaders in their desire to disciple their people in prayer and to become a "house of prayer for all nations." Its online store, prayershop.org, has more than 150 prayer resources available for purchase or download.

ISBN (Print): 978-1-970176-23-0
ISBN (E-Book): 978-1-970176-24-7

1 2 3 4 5 | 2027 2026 2025 2024 2023

CONTENTS

Part 4: A Christ-Awakening

Part 5: Watchmen on the Wall.

Part 6: End Times Urgency

FOREWORD

HAVE YOU EVER SEEN something happen that was truly extraordinary? Unexplainable? Even supernatural? So astonishingly delightful you long to see it again?

In the realm of sports, it's happened to me on two occasions. The first time was my first-ever collegiate basketball game. I can remember exactly where I was sitting. Notre Dame beat the UCLA Bruins, ending the longest winning streak in college hoops: 88 games.

The other was my first-ever professional golf tournament. It was the granddaddy of them all: The Masters. I can remember exactly where I was sitting. I watched . . . not one . . . not two . . . but three hole-in-ones. If that is not enough, all three hole-in-ones were on the same hole the same day. The crowd went crazy. In utter amazement, I was jumping and cheering and hugging people I had never met.

I immensely enjoyed those experiences. But after experiencing them once, I said to myself both times, "Why would I ever attend again? This is as good as it gets."

But the opposite is true with revival. Once you have seen the fire of revival, you long to see it again. And you are never satisfied. You always want more, *until* . . . "the earth is filled with the knowledge of the glory of the LORD" (Hab. 2:14).

I remember where I was sitting when I saw my first-ever extraordinary work of God's Spirit. It was in a city of 45,000 people. For three days, the manifest presence of God hovered above and, then, unmistakably came down and showed up in that community. The stories became like a magnet to my soul, captivating my heart and intensifying my cries for more.

> *An out-of-town salesman approached the city limits sign and was immediately struck by the conviction of God. He stopped on the side of the road, and there he repented of sin after sin. When he arrived in town, he stopped at a gas station and asked the attendant, "Is there something going on in this place?" The unbelieving gas station worker replied, "Don't you know? God is here!"*

> *The president of a bank was overwhelmed by the conviction of the Holy Spirit while sitting at his desk. He went outside and walked up and down the sidewalk until he found someone who could lead him to Christ. He and his entire family came to faith that week, and for the past 40+ years, Mr. Duerstock has been directly involved in Kingdom work, seeing thousands come to Christ.*

I was only 25 years old at the time. After a one-year stint on a revival team, I was planning to leave to continue my business career. But the "fire" experience changed everything. I recall saying to myself, "I would spend the rest of my life just to see this remarkable visitation of God happen one more time." Being in God's presence was something I could not get enough of. So for the past half-century, I have been asking God to "do it again." I am not alone. The psalmist earnestly prayed for God to "do it again."

If that is your longing, you are not alone. There is a growing movement of believers who are issuing forth that simple, yet profoundly powerful cry . . . *Do it again!*

This call is being heralded by each of the authors in this book. I know them. I have served with many of them. I have stood with them, heart-to-heart, asking God for another divine visitation. They have one thing in common: They are united in crying out, *"Lord, do it again."*

Will you join these authors for the next 30 days? And will you, like the sons of Korah, say, "Revive us, again"? Make it personal. Draw a circle (in your heart) and step inside of it and pray, *"Lord, send revival **again**. And let it begin in me!"*

–Byron Paulus,
Founder OneCry

INTRODUCTION

I'VE EDITED MORE THAN 50 issues of *Prayer Connect* magazine, and the consistent underlying themes are bold and confident prayer, hope for revival of the Church, and a vision for spiritual awakening in our nation to the glory of Christ.

That's because the members of our editorial team have devoted ourselves for years to pray with hope in an increasingly dark nation and world. It is ingrained in our spiritual DNA that our desperate need is a supernatural, all-powerful, God-inspired movement that changes hearts, draws people into the Kingdom, and transforms communities into places that reflect the love and truth of Christ.

Will God grant us one more nation-shaking, world-transforming move of His Spirit? Will we experience one more Great Awakening that results in a massive spiritual harvest of souls? Will the Church be revived to live in the fullness of Christ and the unmatched power of the Holy Spirit?

Or is the next thing on the docket the Lord's return and the end of time?

We don't know. But we can pray with faith, hope, and belief that we will see at least one more spectacular move of God before Jesus returns. Our world needs us to pray that way.

Throughout more than a decade of *Prayer Connect* magazine's existence, we have invited godly, spiritually discerning prayer leaders to write on the topic of revival and spiritual awakening. This book is a compilation of excerpts from their contributions. I've added prayer points so that as you glean from their insights, you can also pray a hope-filled response.

I love the faith-filled prayers of Elijah. In 1 Kings 18:41–46, Elijah tells King Ahab to get ready for rain after three years of drought. Then Elijah heads up a mountain with his servant to pray for God to unleash the blessings of heaven. He bows in humble, contending, faith-filled prayer—and then sends his servant out seven times to look for the rain clouds. Six times the servant sees nothing, but then on the seventh search of the skies, he sees a small cloud on the horizon that eventually bursts into a torrential downpour.

I liken that to hope-filled revival praying: Nothing, nothing, nothing, nothing, nothing, nothing . . . *everything!*

The Lord can do it again. We don't know when the breakthrough of revival might come. It might be your next prayer that unleashes everything. Pray like you believe that!

– Carol Madison
Editor, *Prayer Connect* magazine

Part 1

HISTORICAL PERSPECTIVE OF REVIVAL

WE'VE BEEN HERE BEFORE

By Bob Bakke

HOPELESS OR DESPERATE? Prayer dies without a vision of what God can do, has done, and is willing to do. One of the ways we build confidence in our praying is to tell stories. God commanded the Jews to faithfully observe the feasts so that they would not forget His acts of salvation.

Well, we have stories here in America, too. Stories of how desperation resulted in mighty moves of God.

The first and greatest national experience of the newly constituted United States was a massive spiritual awakening in the face of overwhelming problems. Yet we have forgotten this.

The after-effects of the eight years of war for our Independence from England were profound. The 1790s were years of grave national doubts and empty churches. We faced the enormous pressures from superpowers on our borders and the constant threat of renewed war. We teetered on the edge of national bankruptcy.

Plagues killed thousands of our citizens. The nation's harvests were devastated by disease.

Then, there were the philosophical diseases. Our historic colleges—established to train clergy—had few confessing believers. Bibles were publicly burned on campuses.

Political rancor was fed by newspapers owned by political parties.

The editorial pages and cartoons of that period are among the most vicious in American history. Adding to the political rancor was the nastiest presidential election in U.S. history between John Adams and Thomas Jefferson, thought by many as a political struggle for the soul and future of America.

Many churches were empty. Pastors wrote that these were the worst times imagined. Others wrote of about "coarse sensuality" throughout the country.

But then something significant happened. The pastors began a covenant of united prayer.

After years of seeking God, a spiritual explosion took place in 1801 that went through our nation like a wildfire. The revival was so powerful as it swept in every direction that Vanderbilt University historian Paul Conklin called it "America's Pentecost."

It changed the course of world history. Hundreds of denominations were born, thousands of churches were founded, modern missions exploded, college campuses were revived, and tract and Bible societies were established. The abolition of slavery fixed itself to the American soul.

The awakening infiltrated every area of American life. It was a harvest of righteousness that fundamentally changed our culture in a few short years and spun out for nearly 50 years.

In the midst of similar problems today, pray with hope and confidence. We have been here before. We have seen the glory of Christ and its astonishing effects.

Let's not forget.

PRAYER POINTS:

- Ask God to stir in you a vision of what this nation could look like if another Great Awakening were to sweep our land. Pray for the fulfillment of that vision.

- If you have felt discouraged about the negative discourse in our nation, pray for a renewal of hope. Ask God to use you as a conveyor of that hope as you pray with others.
- Pray for a renewed "harvest of righteousness" in our nation.
- Pray for a revival in our day that changes the course of world history.
- Pray that your church will be filled with intercessors who will join you in praying with hope for another Great Awakening.

AN ANCIENT PATTERN FOR REVIVAL

By Dan and Melissa Jarvis

I F YOU KNEW GOD only wanted you to do two things before blessing you with a revival of His presence—would you do them?

What if they required real sacrifice? A rearrangement of priorities? What if you'd have to give up things in your life, your household, your relationships, and even in your future?

The Bible is full of such calls to absolute commitment: "deny yourself and follow me," "give up everything you have," "sell your possessions and give to the poor," or even "pray without ceasing." So, what if the road to revival is paved with the same kind of surrender—radical, full-life obedience?

Old Testament history reads like a textbook for revival. We find many examples of wayward souls returning to God, from individuals to an entire nation. And, upon study of these spiritual transformations, a pattern emerges—not a "formula," not "revival in a bottle," but a pattern that holds true 100 percent of the time.

Every time God moves to restore His people, *every* time there is a fresh wind of blessing and power in their midst—two components emerge.

First, something had to be destroyed. Then worship had to commence. From Jacob to Ezra, when Israel was called to return to God's

17

DO IT AGAIN, LORD!

love and God's law, they first obliterated their idols. Then they set out to worship with the best of their music, architecture, prayer, and obedience. Revival wasn't just a theory or a theme or a set of special meetings, *it was a new life and new commitment that changed everything.*

Can we pray for this sort of spiritual transformation today? Times are different, to be sure. God's people and God's plan look very different from the ancient monarchy of Israel. But the principles of revival still ring true, do they not? Are we still tempted to cling to idols, holding back the best of our worship from God? Do we still look for security in earthly things, setting them up as "gods" we hold in high esteem?

Let's destroy our idols, worship God with all we have, and pray for revival!

PRAYER POINTS:

- Praise God that it is His heart to restore His people and pour out a fresh blessing of His presence.
- Ask God to reveal the idols in your life and in our nation that need to be destroyed.
- Ask for a renewed commitment to sacrifice that moves you and other believers to radical, full-life obedience.
- Pray for a revival of pure, God-focused worship throughout the Church in this nation.
- Pray for an outpouring of revival and spiritual awakening that results in new life and transformation of churches and communities.

HE CAN DO IT AGAIN

By Jim Jarman

SOMETIMES PRAYER DOESN'T just precede a revival. Sometimes prayer *is* the revival.

It seemed to be a normal Tuesday in February 1970, when students at Asbury College in Kentucky filed into Hughes Auditorium at 10:00 a.m. for their regular, required chapel service. Some, however, sensed the presence of the Spirit upon entering—almost as if the room was being transformed into holy ground.

The school's academic dean was in charge of the service that day. He decided not to preach, but instead gave his testimony and then invited the students to come and share what God was doing in their lives. One student came, followed by another and then another. The 50-minute chapel service lasted 185 hours non-stop, 24 hours a day. It was not planned in advance. There was no predominant leader. No one wanted to leave.

Students were weeping, publicly confessing their sins, praying in small groups, seeking out and asking forgiveness from others they had wronged. Some sang quietly in small groups. Everyone was polite and orderly.

As students prayed that week, they sensed the Spirit telling them to take the revival to other schools. Teams were formed and during the first week of travel, students went to churches and schools in 16 states and saw more than 1,000 conversions. By the summer of 1970, teams had gone to some 130 other colleges, seminaries, and Bible schools from New York to California to Latin America. Everywhere they went, revival followed. Weeping. Repentance. Conversions. Prayer.

I personally experienced this renewal because my college was one of the first schools that the Asbury teams visited. My life has never been the same. When my own personal hope seems to vanish, I remember what God did in the past and what He has done for me.

Arms raised. Knees bowed. Face down. Hearts broken. It is never too late to ask the God who longs to redeem to do the seemingly impossible. There is a renewed sense of hope that God might answer our prayers for revival in the nations of the earth. By His Spirit, He is stirring His people to pray in greater numbers than ever before. If Jesus is still interceding for us, how can we possibly stop praying for others?

What God has done in the past, He can do again. This is the hope we have for our nations, cities, friends, and loved ones.

PRAYER POINTS:

- Praise God that He is the same faithful God today as He is of the past.
- Praise Jesus that He continues to intercede for you, your church, and our nation. Pray that He inspires even greater prayer in you.
- Pray for a movement of confession and repentance across campuses in our nation today. Ask God to do it again!
- Pray for renewed hope in your own heart that no matter how dire or dark it appears, God has no limits in how He might break through in revival.
- Ask the God who redeems to do the impossible in your family and the next generation.

THERE'S SOMETHING MORE

By Carol Madison

THERE ARE LOTS of things we can pray for: protection for family members, salvation of unsaved loved ones, healing of the sick, marriages restored, the next generation to stay true to the faith. But is there something more?

Yes, God desires so much more for His people! He longs to see His Church revived and His people become agents of transformation in their communities.

One of my favorite revival stories comes from the Hebrides Islands off the coast of Scotland during the years of 1948–50. A couple of home-bound elderly sisters, one who was blind and the other who was severely hampered by arthritis, were instrumental through their prayers. The sisters, grieved by the decline of the church in their community and especially by the lack of interest among the young people, prayed faithfully, often late into the night. God implanted a vision for revival in their hearts, and they began to cry out with faith and hope.

As the leaders of the church joined in prayer, God began to move in tangible and powerful ways. The pastor and elders repented before God and humbled themselves in desperation for their community. In one of the prayer meetings, it was reported that the home shook, much like in the Book of Acts (see Acts 4:31).

The presence of God descended upon their community and surrounding villages throughout the Hebrides. Stories emerged of people coming under such strong conviction of the Holy Spirit that they fell to their knees in the streets, begging forgiveness. Eventually, no village was left untouched by the presence of God.

It all started with the faith and conviction of two sisters who simply offered themselves and their prayers as catalysts for revival!

Many factors can be involved in a move of revival in a church and spiritual awakening in a community, but it can also begin with just a handful of people whose hearts are committed to seeing God's glory manifested in their own streets.

The formula is simple, but the calling is dramatic and selfless. God's people must humble themselves in prayer with their eyes fixed on the Lord, their hearts desperate for His presence, a willingness to repent and turn from sin, and a belief that God is not only capable but willing to "heal our land" (2 Chron. 7:14).

When God calls His people to pray, I believe it's because He intends to answer that prayer!

PRAYER POINTS:

- Praise God that He responds to the prayers of His people and delights in displaying His glory.
- Humble yourself before the Lord, invite Him to reveal ways you need to repent, and ask Him to bring you into alignment with His Kingdom plans.
- Pray that you will be a prayer catalyst for revival—and will inspire others to pray with faith and boldness.
- Ask the Spirit to prompt your church to pray with a 2 Chronicles 7:14 vision of seeing your city and nation healed in the truth and power of Jesus.
- Pray for the revival of your church, the spiritual awakening of the lost, and the transformation of your community.

Part 2

HUMILITY
AND
REPENTANCE

OUR SIN IS GREAT

By David Kubal

THE SIN OF OUR NATION IS GREAT. We have killed more than 60 million innocent babies. In 2015 the Supreme Court used its power to "redefine" the institution of marriage, which God created to be the building block of humanity. Pornography is prolific. And in some jurisdictions, a male may walk into a women's restroom if he feels like a female, thus threatening the modesty, privacy, and security of women and young girls

Instead of expecting revival, we Christians should expect divine discipline. We cry out, "Bless us, oh, Lord," while instead we should be prostrating ourselves, crying out in repentance. We expect God to bring revival, even when we do not value His truth.

Perhaps God has not brought revival to our county for the very reason that we expect it. There is no remorse. We are not sorry in a way that matches the level of our collective guilt. We don't need intercessors for America as much as we need mourners for America.

As Isaiah looked at his nation, he understood the depths of the depravity of his day. He didn't cry out, "Lord, bring Your blessing." He cried out, "Woe to me! . . . I am ruined!" (Isa. 6:5).

Isaiah was shaken to his core with the sight of God's holiness and his own brokenness. His only response: "I am a man of unclean lips, and I live among a people of unclean lips, and my eyes have seen the King, the Lord Almighty" (6:5).

Is it possible that God has not brought revival to our county because we expect Him to do so, as though we were entitled to that grace? Perhaps God is waiting for His people to show greater remorse and repentance on behalf of the nation. The larger Church also appears to lack deep contrition. Historically, intercession has included a sense of mourning over our personal and collective sins.

Can you imagine what would happen in this country if the Church came together with holy hands, sacrificial fasting, and the worship of God in a way that brought unity and a desire only for God's glory? This is what it takes for a nation to be healed. Repentant, desperate prayer is what it will take for certain blessings to be released.

Let us remember that God holds nations accountable. And let's approach Him with an accurate understanding of our guilt before Him, realizing He desires us to join Him in shaping history through prayer.

Prayer Points:

- Humbly acknowledge God's unsurpassable holiness—and our brokenness in His presence. He is good and just in all He does.
- Ask God to wake up His Church to be obedient in her role of mourning for the sins of our nation and repenting before our holy God.
- Pray that your church will embrace hearts of contrition, sacrificial fasting, and other ways to demonstrate deep humility before God.
- Pray for healing of this nation through repentant, desperate prayer that changes the course of history.
- Pray for God's mercy to release undeserved blessing upon this nation that results in multitudes turning to Christ.

TRUTHS TO REMEMBER

By David Kubal

"IT JUST MAKES my blood boil."

These are the words I heard coming out of my own mouth at a prayer event—in front of a bunch of people—when I described the latest political "breaking news."

Then the Spirit reminded me that anger is reserved for God.

Holding onto anger against someone for their unrighteous acts gets us nowhere. It just makes us bitter. The very people I want to be angry with are individuals like me, created in God's image, created with purpose, created with a destiny. But they have not yet found the purpose and destiny God has designed for them. As I try to adopt that perspective, I have actually begun to forgive them. And forgiveness releases me from anger.

The Church has a great opportunity, summed up in three prayer points:

1. Pray prayers resulting in peace. Paul says in 1 Timothy 2:1–2, "I urge, then, *first of all*, that petitions, prayers, intercession and thanksgiving be made for all people—for kings and all those in authority, that we may live peaceful and quiet lives in all godliness and holiness" (emphasis added). These verses remind us of our primary prayer priority and give us an outcome to pursue. We are to first pray for our government leaders *so that* we can live peaceful, godly, holy lives.

2. Pray prayers reflecting God's sovereignty. Psalm 2:1–5 declares, "Why do the nations conspire and the peoples plot in vain?

The kings of the earth rise up and the rulers band together against the Lord and against his anointed. . . . The One enthroned in heaven laughs; the Lord scoffs at them. He rebukes them in his anger and terrifies them in his wrath."

Remember, ultimately the course of our nation is up to God. He will have His way. When we understand God's sovereignty, we have peace, and our civil engagement can be a joyful act of obedience instead of a desperate attempt to save our nation before we lose it.

3. Pray prayers of praise. The psalmist writes, "May the peoples praise you, God; may all the peoples praise you. May the nations be glad and sing for joy, for you rule the peoples with equity and guide the nations of the earth. May the peoples praise you, God; may all the peoples praise you. The land yields its harvest; God, our God, blesses us" (Ps. 67:3–6).

A nation that expresses gratitude on a large scale will be blessed by God.

We can't afford to let anything make our blood boil. God wants us to get rid of anger, remain levelheaded, and pray prayers of peace—all the while praising His sovereignty and His provision.

PRAYER POINTS:

- Praise God that He is just and that He alone possesses righteous anger over sin. Pray for humility to understand your own sinfulness in the presence of His holiness.
- Pray for a release of forgiveness in God's people that inspires them to pray for the salvation and transformation of unrighteous people.
- Pray for all governmental authorities to lead in ways that instill peace in our communities and nation.
- Pray for increased trust in God's sovereignty that brings you peace and confidence in your civil engagement.
- Pray that our nation will be glad, sing for joy, and express our gratitude to our sovereign God.

WHEN GOD'S PRESENCE INVADES

By Doug Small

OUR GENERATION HAS NEVER seen a Great Awakening, but previous generations have witnessed transformed communities. It can happen again. Yet, all we do—praying, living in caring relationships, and sharing the gospel—will fall short unless God comes to town.

Remember: *Community impact* is dependent on a *healthy spiritual community*, and that is dependent on the quality of the *unity*, which is in turn dependent on the depth and sincerity of our *humility*. All of this rises from our ongoing, consistent exposure to *God's holiness* and *sovereignty*—in prayer—both individually and corporately.

The prince of darkness is here. An evil force is determined to invade our land. At some point we will find ourselves at the threshold of the ultimate battle foretold in Scripture—an unavoidable war that cannot be averted.

But God calls us to take a stand now or lose our cities. We must not shrink back. We need to mobilize ongoing prayer—watchman prayer—that will never be finished. Should God grant us another Great Awakening, millions will be saved and brought into His Kingdom. Even though we cannot divert the coming storm of end times, we must have a prayerful and systematic commitment to fulfill the Great Commission.

When an "awakening" occurs in a community, God is *unavoidable*.

The heightened God-consciousness is evident even among unbelievers, especially those who were previously the least likely to become believers. God changes hearts.

There is no arguing with God. Rather, there is conviction, a renewed reverence—a fear of God. Simultaneously His compelling love draws people to Him. They cry out to Him spontaneously. Salvations occur by the dozens, then the hundreds and thousands. It is God who breaks addictive behavior patterns. It is God who restores marriages. It is God who recalibrates decency and morality. It is God who shifts cultural appetites to the spiritual. Church attendance soars. Ungodly establishments shut down. And we stand in awe of our holy God.

Is there hope for genuine community transformation? Yes—if we, in desperation, truly see God in His holiness and sovereignty, if we, in desperation, seek *Him* more than a *plan*, and if we, in desperation, humble ourselves to pray and work in unity for His glory.

That will be God-coming-to-town transformation!

PRAYER POINTS:

- Praise God that His manifest presence is unavoidable and His compelling love draws people to Him.
- Invite God to awaken you and your church to the prince of darkness, evil forces, and the spiritual battle that consumes our land. Pray that your response will be bold prayer instead of fear and intimidation.
- Pray for a renewed reverence for God in the Church that will bring people to humble dependence on the Lord for transformation of cities and our nation.
- Pray for a move of God that inspires salvations, restored marriages, freedom from addictions, and a return to decency and morality.
- Pray that you will witness a God-coming-to-town transformation in your own community as you seek God in humble desperation.

REPENTERS REPENT

By Byron Paulus

COULD IT BE THAT the single greatest deterrent to revival in our day is that Christians have stopped repenting? When was the last time *you* genuinely repented of your sin? Not just asked forgiveness but consciously repented? Or at least recognized the necessity of a heart attitude of repentance?

Oswald Chambers has called repentance "the bedrock of Christianity." I believe the failure of the Church to understand and embrace the biblical concept of repentance has robbed us of the glory of God in our midst. The revival we pray and believe God for will grant us must be birthed in genuine repentance.

Some years ago, I heard Josef Tson, then in exile from Romania, relate the events that led up to the revival that swept through his homeland in the 1970s. In Romania, evangelical believers of various denominations are known as "repenters." This designation is commonly used because of the emphasis placed on repentance at the time of conversion.

At the Second Baptist Church in Oradea, where the revival began, God placed a pastor who challenged his people regarding their need for repentance. For six months, his message was, "It is time for the 'repenters' to repent!"

He called them to repent in several specific matters; among them, the fact that many of the believers in that area (known for its wine vineyards) were themselves indulging.

Furthermore, many Christians were involved in the commonly accepted practice of stealing from the lands that the Communists had confiscated from the people. This pastor called for his people to repent of these and other practices, and to enter into a covenant not to be conformed to the world around them.

The "repenters" repented. And when they did, God began to unleash the power of His Spirit in an extraordinary way that has continued to this day. Ultimately, God used the revived Church in Romania to provide the spiritual and moral impetus for the Revolution that released that country from the tyranny of Communist oppression.

And so, as always, repentance gave birth to freedom. Even today, repenters must repent if we hope to see revival.

PRAYER POINTS:

- Praise God that He uses the humble hearts of His people to unleash His power to transformation nations.
- Invite God to reveal attitudes of your heart that can be a deterrent to your own personal revival.
- Ask the Lord to convict you by His Spirit of any sin. Pray that you will be quick to repent and be reconciled to Him.
- Pray that God will use your repentant heart as an encouragement to others to walk in a lifestyle of repentance.
- Pray that as a "repenter who repents," God will unleash the power of His Spirit in your church and nation.

PATHWAY TO REVIVAL

By Byron Paulus

OVER A DECADE AGO, pollster George Gallup, Jr. observed that most Americans who profess Christianity don't act significantly different from non-Christians in their daily lives. What would a similar survey reveal today?

This indictment only underscores the need for a new cry to be heard throughout the Church of our land: "It is time for the repenters to repent!"

Of course, the call to repentance must be heard by those whose sin is blatant and known to all. But the first to respond to this message ought to be those of us in positions of spiritual leadership and influence. We are the ones who must lead the way in repentance, brokenness, and humility. Then we must lead those who follow us into a lifestyle of continuous repentance. That is the pathway of continuous revival.

Consider this eternal reality. When the God of this universe determined to introduce the physical ministry of His Son Jesus here on earth, He chose John the Baptist as the messenger—and repentance as the message. Why? As the psalmist said, "Righteousness goes as a herald before him, preparing the way for his steps" (Ps. 85:13, NLT).

Should it be any different today? As we seek God for His manifest presence by way of His Spirit in revival, could it be the only reason God has not chosen to descend is because we have not chosen to repent?

In the deepest parts of my heart, I long for the day when God shows up, when "the earth [is] filled with the knowledge of the glory of the LORD as the waters cover the sea" (Hab. 2:14). What an amazing gift that will be!

But should we not view repentance as an amazing gift as well? Is the means to the end not also glorious? Should we not ask God to express His kindness (Rom. 2:4) by giving a spirit of repentance? God delights in giving repentance, but do I delight in asking Him for it?

Allow God to examine *your own heart* in relation to this matter. Ask Him to personalize these truths to *your life*, and to enable *you* to enter into a richer, deeper level of personal repentance.

Then ask God to grant His Church the gift of repentance. A repenting Church will be a revived Church. And only a revived Church can reveal the glory of God to a darkened world.

Prayer Points

- Praise God for His promise that one day the earth will be filled with the knowledge of His glory.
- Praise Jesus for His message and gift of repentance that opens the door for our reconciliation with God.
- Ask God to examine your heart and reveal any ways you need to repent and seek a deeper relationship with Him.
- Thank God for the hopeful pathway to revival through the gift of repentance to His Church.
- Pray for a revived Church that brings the light and glory of Christ to a lost world.

WHEN GOD DOESN'T RESPOND

By Bill Elliff

MANY BELIEVERS TODAY are getting desperate. Seeing the moral and spiritual free fall in the world around us and the declining condition of the Church in our land drives us to cry out to God. We need Him. We need His manifest presence. We need revival in the Church and spiritual awakening among the unbelieving. We need our nation to be restored to its Kingdom calling as a mighty, gospel-sending station to the world.

According to Scripture, the precursor to any great movement of God is always humble, repentant prayer. We thank God that people across the country are praying in record numbers.

But wouldn't it be tragic to discover that our prayers are not effective? Wouldn't it be heartbreaking to learn that some things in our lives prevent our prayers from accomplishing what is so desperately needed? Wouldn't it be devastating to find out that all our hard work in prayer is doing nothing to advance the Kingdom?

While Scripture contains hundreds of positive promises regarding answered prayer, God also outlines many things that will hinder our prayers. No one prays perfectly, and God is not playing with us. He does not make intercession so unattainable that only the super-spiritual can be effective. He understands our weakness. But He is also very clear about those things that can hinder our prayers.

Are we willing to evaluate the effectiveness of our prayer lives? And when God shows us areas of need, we can turn to Him in repentance and take the necessary steps to adjust our lives to encounter Him afresh in prayer.

Several years ago, I found myself in a very dry time—bland Bible study and hindered prayers. Worst of all, my love for Christ had grown cold. I felt God calling me to spend an extended time in fasting, simply to lay aside everything that was clouding my heart so I could hear Him.

The Lord peeled back layers of sin and showed me ways I had been disregarding Him. He began to speak to me in new ways through His Word. He placed fresh, heaven-sent prayers into my soul. I fell in love with Him all over again.

Not long after this time, God answered one of the great prayers of my heart and sent a mighty work of revival to the church I pastored. That revival lasted five weeks, three to four hours every night. I do not pretend that my solitary prayers, once rightly aligned, brought revival. But I know that He prepared my heart for what He was about to accomplish. And I know He was graciously initiating and answering prayer afresh in my life.

PRAYER POINTS:

- Praise God that He established this nation with a Kingdom calling to spread the gospel to the world.
- Praise God for how the Spirit is calling more people to pray for revival and spiritual awakening.
- Pray that your church will be fully engaged in seeking God for a fresh movement of His Spirit throughout our nation.
- Pray for evidence of revival in your church that causes people to pray with greater faith and belief. Pray for an outpouring of the Spirit!
- Pray that you will encounter Jesus in fresh ways in prayer that are reviving and restoring.

Part 3

HOPE-FILLED
PRAYERS

RIPE FOR REVIVAL

By Bob Bakke

TROUBLES ARE BUFFETING our nation. Respected voices say that our nation, as it was conceived, is lost, and the American Church forever diminished.

In spite of these voices—and without being Pollyannaish—I count myself among those who see the U.S. as ripe for revival and spiritual awakening. I've studied the often-grizzly stories of Church history. I personally experienced the riots, the burned-out cities, the assassinations, the threat of nuclear war, and massive political upheavals of the 1960s. Yet, in the midst of tragic times throughout history, we have had many awakenings in our land—both in the colonial period and since our nation's founding.

God's people are being rattled from their small, distracted, complacent, and lackadaisical faith. They are being confronted in their sin, perhaps as a separating of the wheat from the chaff (Matt. 3:11–12).

While God's people need a fresh wind of the Spirit to enliven, embolden, and refine their faith [revival], an unbelieving world is realizing they need God [spiritual awakening]. This sounds like a confluence ripe for God's intervention, and I think we are seeing evidences of such.

What might spiritual awakening look like in our day?

Let's keep it simple. Act 1–2 reveals the qualities present whenever the Spirit revives His people and awakens the lost. In Jerusalem, Pentecost's transforming power of the Spirit on His people arose out of sustained and earnest prayer. The transformation produced powerful preaching. That preaching resulted in profound repentance and faith. And that profound faith launched and sustained a radical way of life that impacted every facet of the city.

There are hopeful signs of a coming spiritual awakening. We should be deeply impressed with the quantity and quality of prayer being mobilized across our nation. The bride of Christ is waking up to the dangers in front of her. A unity, unlike any in previous generations, is forming. This unity is diverse, multiethnic, and multinational. The one thing missing, however, is vision. I believe God will provide it, but we must pray for that united vision.

I believe we are, indeed, ripe for revival and spiritual awakening. Let's ask God to give us the vision to see what its fulfillment would look like. And let's ask God to give leaders the wisdom to embrace it.

PRAYER POINTS:

- Praise God that there is always hope for another Great Awakening in our nation! Ask God to inspire your prayers with belief that it is His heart to do it again.
- Praise God for how He is alerting His Church to pray with unity and urgency for a coming spiritual awakening. Pray for your leaders to embrace such a vision.
- Pray through Acts 1–2 by paying attention to the ways the Holy Spirit poured out life and power to the Church. Ask Him to do it again.
- Pray that your church will be inspired to lift up hopeful prayers that go beyond distracted and complacent faith.
- Pray for a vision of prayer for revival that is diverse, multiethnic, and multinational.

YET WE HAVE HOPE

By Kay Horner

TYPICALLY, WE WOULDN'T turn to Lamentations—a book of poetic laments—to revitalize our hope. We might read a few psalms for a good "pick-me-up." But we may forget that the Old Testament hymns and poems contain more laments than praise psalms.

In fact, the writer of Psalm 42 asks a question that Jesus' followers, in every generation, face during difficult times: "Why, my soul, are you downcast? Why so disturbed within me?" (v. 5). Aren't we supposed to rejoice always and be victorious through Christ?

In the same verse, in the middle of bemoaning his troubles, the psalmist inserts the secret for reigniting our prayer and praise when disappointments seem insurmountable: "Put your hope in God, for I will yet praise him, my Savior and my God."

Jeremiah, the probable author of Lamentations, may have remembered this psalm as he grieved the destruction of Jerusalem and other afflictions. He offers the consummate answer to life's dilemmas—*hope in God!*

The weeping prophet then defines the anchor of our hope as the Lord's infinite love, unfailing compassions, and abounding faithfulness.

> This I call to mind and therefore I have hope:
> Because of the Lord's great love we are not consumed,
> for his compassions never fail.

> They are new every morning;
> great is your faithfulness (Lam. 3:21–23).

Jeremiah continues by recounting the *whys* for his hope. He then challenges himself and the people of Zion to examine their ways, return to the Lord, and acknowledge their sin (vv. 25–42).

When divisiveness pervades a nation, this bright picture of repentance and hope, against the dark backdrop of despair, becomes a starting point for prayer. Even when the doors of prayer seem tightly shut, the foyer of weeping is always open.

The prophet's hope confronts his sorrows. Faith debates fears. Night or day, the Lord God of heaven and earth demonstrates His extravagant kindness and inexhaustible faithfulness. God's covenant love always wins the argument!

Prayer Points:

- Praise God that we can always put our hope in Him as our Savior and Lord!
- Praise the Lord that His great love keeps us from being consumed, and His unfailing compassions are new every morning!
- Ask God to renew your prayer and praise, even amid disappointments that may seem insurmountable in our nation.
- Pray for a spirit of weeping and repentance to overcome the Church as a prelude to revival.
- Pray for a nation-transforming demonstration of God's extravagant kindness and inexhaustible faithfulness.

UNFOLDING STORY OF HOPE

By Kay Horner

WAIT IS AN UGLY, four-letter word to most of us. Our Internet-speed expectations avoid waiting at any cost. However, the original word for *hope* in Lamentations 3:21 can be translated *wait*.

Times of waiting strengthen our character. And the Lord reveals *His* character as He pours His love into and out of our hearts.

The apostle Paul experienced intense, personal suffering, and he ministered during a season of religious divisiveness and governmental persecution. At that time, Jesus' followers in Rome could have easily despaired if they had not put their hope in the love of God. Yet Paul knew the secret and the cycle of hope:

> Since we have been justified through faith, we have peace with God through our Lord Jesus Christ, through whom we have gained access by faith into this grace in which we now stand. And we boast in the hope of the glory of God. Not only so, but we also glory in our sufferings, because we know that suffering produces perseverance; perseverance, character; and character, hope. And hope does not put us to shame, because God's love has been poured out into our hearts through the Holy Spirit, who has been given to us (Rom. 5:1–5).

Are we hoping for national tranquility, church/ministry growth, or relief from our suffering? Or is our hope that "the earth will be filled with the knowledge of the glory of the LORD as the waters cover the sea" (Hab. 2:14)?

Anyone who has ever dealt with a water leak or flooding knows the power of water. It diffuses, seeps, and pours through the tiniest opening. In a similar way God's overflowing, abundant love can permeate every area of our lives so that we won't give up hope in crushing times. Paul uses a verb tense here that indicates an action in the past with results continuing to the present. What a great way to emphasize the abundance of God's love!

Paul wasn't focusing on tranquility of the heart but on a relationship with God. We may feel more like lamenting than rejoicing in our suffering, but God tells us to persevere and to allow Him to lovingly transform our character through repentant prayer and grateful worship.

Ultimately, we will always cycle back to hope when we recall with Jeremiah and Paul that God's compassions never fail, and He continually pours His love into our lives.

PRAYER POINTS:

- Praise God for the ways He strengthens you and reveals His character in your times of waiting.
- Pray that in your suffering, God will renew your hope and peace in Christ. Ask Him to use your life for His glory.
- Invite God to fill the earth with the knowledge of His glory— even in our day!
- Pray that God's overflowing and abundant love will permeate every area of your life—and be a witness to others of hope in Christ.
- Pray for a deepening relationship with Jesus that gives you hope to persevere and faith to pray for revival and spiritual awakening.

HOPE DEFERRED

By Jim Jarman

Hope can be defined as *the belief or expectation that something can or will happen.* Proverbs 13:12 describes it this way: "Hope deferred makes the heart sick, but a longing fulfilled is a tree of life."

How do we pray when hope seems lost, when a situation deteriorates rather than comes to resolution? How can we keep from becoming discouraged and giving up when our nation slips further and further into darkness? How do we maintain confidence in the grace and love of God when judgment, logical consequences, and the downward slope of destruction seem inevitable?

Let's face it: Isn't it difficult to maintain endurance in our prayer lives—to intercede for years only to see no progress, or worse, regression? Prayer is often described as a battle—a fight we sometimes wonder if we're losing. God told the prophet Jeremiah to stop praying for Israel (Jer. 14:11–12) because in His displeasure, He had deemed it was too late. He was sending judgment.

Should we do the same when it seems our nation also deserves judgment? When hope for revival is deferred or other prayer longings go unanswered, it doesn't just make our hearts sick. It also makes our guts wrench, our muscles weak, and our minds confused.

Prayer is supposed to be offered up in faith. But if faith is the "assurance of things hoped for" (Heb. 11:1, ESV), what do we do when our hope is gone?

We often give up hoping for our own self-preservation. If we don't dream, then we won't be disappointed. If we want to play catch with Dad, but Dad's always working, eventually we decide baseball isn't so important. If we long for revival, yet we don't see repentance on the horizon, we believe our prayers for revival are wasted.

There is a reason Paul reminded the Church at Rome: "May the God of hope fill you with all joy and peace as you trust in him, so that you may overflow with hope by the power of the Holy Spirit" (Rom. 15:13). The God of hope wants us to overflow with hope, but it will require the power of the Spirit in our lives.

Just imagine: complete joy, total peace, and an abundance of hope! Isn't that what we need?

PRAYER POINTS:

- Praise the God of hope who pours out joy and peace when we trust in Him.
- Pray for renewed endurance in your prayer life to keep interceding even when you don't see immediate evidence of revival.
- Pray for God's mercy on our nation, even when it seems judgment is more appropriate.
- Ask God to increase your faith and inspire your prayers with "the assurance of things hoped for."
- Pray for a wave of repentance and a flood of revival throughout the Church in this nation.

PRAYING GOD'S PURPOSES

By Dave Butts

OUR HEARTS ARE growing increasingly urgent about the need to pray for God's mercy and grace in our country. This is the simple prayer that the Lord put on my heart:

Lord, how would You have me pray for my nation? I watch with horror as we increasingly turn from Your ways. Your precious Word speaks so strongly to our situation: "The wicked freely strut about when what is vile is honored among men" (Ps. 12:8).

The Psalmist David again asks the right question for our day, "When the foundations are being destroyed, what can the righteous do?" (Ps. 11:3).

It is because I love the United States of America that I pray with passion for her. Lord, You have greatly blessed our nation. From our beginning, there have been those in leadership who have honored You and sought to lead us in righteousness. You have made us a beacon for freedom around the world for those who are oppressed and downtrodden. The material blessings from Your hand have welled up in national generosity to help those who are hurting, both within and outside our borders.

We recognize our imperfect human nature and structures. While fighting for freedom, we had periods of slavery within our own nation. Even with slavery behind us, freedom was not always available to all in the same measure. The list of our sins, Lord, is long. Without

Your mercy, who could stand?

Throughout our nation's history You have blessed us with times of spiritual awakening and revival. Your Spirit moved in our midst to restore godly worship. You empowered Your people to be witnesses to Your truths and to take stands for righteousness and justice.

Oh, God, do it again! Come upon Your people again in reviving power. Before our nation can be changed, our hearts must be changed. Turn us from selfishness and sin to Your loving ways.

Your Word tells us, Lord, that judgment begins in the house of the Lord (1 Peter 4:17). May Your mercy and grace also begin there. Pour out a spirit of repentance upon the Church in America. Forgive us for making our faith more about us and our comfort and preferences than about Your purposes on planet earth. Fill our pulpits with godly preachers who will proclaim Your Word fearlessly.

We will respond to Your Word as those who are called by Your name, humbling ourselves before You and in prayer, seeking Your face and turning from our wicked ways. Father, will You then hear from heaven and forgive our sin and heal our land (2 Chron. 7:14)?

We ask this in the powerful name of Jesus! Amen.

PRAYER POINTS:

- Praise God for His mercy and the many ways He has blessed our nation.
- Praise God for the way He has used this nation as a beacon of righteousness to the world, and ask Him to use us again to reflect the love of Christ.
- Pray that God will use His Church to be a standard of righteousness and justice in a hurting world.
- Ask God to pour out a spirit of repentance on His Church that paves the way for revival.
- Pray for God's blessing of the fulfillment of 2 Chronicles 7:14.

Part 4

CHRIST-AWAKENING

FULLY ALIVE TO CHRIST'S GLORY

By David Bryant

DEATH VALLEY IS AN expansive desert in California, known as the lowest, driest, and hottest location in all North America. It is a barren, desolate place that holds the record for the highest recorded temperature in the Western Hemisphere—a mere 134 degrees Fahrenheit!

"Death" is obviously a fitting description. Not much survives in Death Valley, whether vegetation or any human life exposed to the elements. But that doesn't necessarily mean life is not possible.

In 2005, a rare torrential downpour deposited six inches of rain into the cracks of the rock-hard valley floor. Suddenly this lifeless desert blossomed with abundant and gorgeous flowers that had not been seen in 20 years! Dormant seeds, sitting underneath the soil for years and barely hanging on to life, were suddenly awakened when saturated with life-giving rain. The desert was alive, much like the promise of Isaiah 44:3–4:

"For I will pour water on the thirsty land, and streams on the dry ground; I will pour out my Spirit on your offspring, and my blessing on your descendants. They will spring up like grass in a meadow, like poplar trees by flowing streams."

This is a picture of revival—when the Spirit saturates a church with God's Word about God's Son so that God's people come alive to His glory in whole new ways.

Revival is more than just an event in a church calendar. When God reenergizes a community of Christians, He intends Kingdom results that last many years. Scholars' research verifies that, following each one of the four so-called "Great Awakenings" in American history (early 1700s, late 1700s, mid 1800s, early 1900s), decades of documented transformations took place both in churches and in society.

God gave His people "fresh winds," not simply to fire up enthusiasm for spiritual things, but also to extend further the reign of His Son within communities and nations through His Church.

PRAYER POINTS:

- Praise God for His heart to pour out water on a dry and thirsty land! Ask Him to do it again with refreshing waters of revival in our day.
- Identify places in your own life, your family, and your church that need an outpouring of God's Spirit—and invite Him to send a torrential downpour!
- Pray for your church to be saturated with God's Word about God's Son—and for your congregation to come alive to the glory of Christ.
- Pray for a Christ awakening that changes both your church and society.
- Pray for fresh winds of the Spirit to extend the reign of Christ to your community and nation.

A LOOK BACK AND FORWARD

By David Bryant

REVIVAL, INTERESTINGLY enough, was a shared experience by saints in both Old and New Testaments. There was a difference, however, between the two eras in how the experience played itself out.

In the Old Testament, the reviving of Israel was usually characterized by a look *back*, as the nation sought to return to previous highwater marks in Israel's religious pilgrimage. Note how Elijah on Mt. Carmel challenged Israel to return to days of spiritual faithfulness before Baal worship had taken over (2 Kings 18). Or recall how Hezekiah refurbished the time-worn temple and reinstituted the ancient Passover tradition, shaping the revival that emerged under his watch.

In the New Testament, however, revival is characterized much more as a look *forward*. It is focused on fresh extensions of Christ's reign among His people and into the world. Consider the prayer meeting of Acts 4: what they prayed, how God answered, and the aftermath in the succeeding stories of missionary advance—all forward-looking.

In a Christ dominated revival, the Holy Spirit increases vision for what's *ahead*. He deepens our yearnings for greater approximations of the coming Kingdom.

In New Testament-style revival, Christians are aroused to a reality of Christ's presence and power already theirs, but currently overlooked.

They are summoned not only to recapture their first love for Christ (Rev. 2), but to discover a passion for Him that surpasses whatever they have known before (Eph. 3). Re-awakening us to greater dimensions of His glory, New Testament revival is ultimately about recovering and enlarging *hope in Christ.*

In other words, God infuses His Church with fresh hope, passion, prayer, and mission by refocusing us on Christ for *ALL* He really is. *In revival a church is re-captivated with the supremacy of Christ by the Spirit of Christ.* That's why my favorite term for this phenomenon is a "Christ Awakening."

PRAYER POINTS:

- Look back both in Scripture and in this nation and praise God for the moves of revival and spiritual awakening that have transformed history.
- Look forward to fresh expressions of Christ's reign and pray that it will happen in our day.
- Invite God to increase your vision and yearning for another Great Awakening in our nation.
- Pray for your church to experience a new awakening of the presence and power of Christ.
- Pray that you and your family will recapture your first love of Christ in ways that transform your relationships.

LONGING FOR CHANGE

By David Kubal

H OW CAN WE, AS intercessors, pray both personally and corporately for transformation? How can we develop a longing for the presence and glory of Christ to flood our communities?

Although the past is set in stone—its events cannot be relived—the future of your city and mine and the future of our nation is not yet determined. Many Christians, however, seem to have only a vague understanding of how God interacts with cities and nations. Both the Old and New Testaments describe this interaction:

• In Genesis, God mandates that men and women become stewards of the land (Gen. 1:28, 2:15). This all-encompassing command means guarding, keeping, protecting, watching over, and retaining God's plan for creation. Even after sin entered the world, He never rescinded His stewardship edict for each one of us.

• In Acts, during Paul's discourse at Athens, he reveals that this divine purpose for mankind continues today: "From one man he [God] made all the nations, that they should inhabit the whole earth; and he marked out their appointed times in history and the boundaries of their lands. God did this so that they would seek him and perhaps reach out for him and find him" (Acts 17:26–27).

Simply put, God made every nation and appointed a place in time for each so that the gospel might go forth. He always intended His people to be involved in shaping history with Him. Many Scripture passages build upon this theme (2 Chron. 7:14; Jer. 18:7–8). Even those people who consider our era to be the "last days" would agree that until the very end, God calls believers to steward the land and its resources for God's glory.

We know that only the gospel's power can change the human heart (Rom. 1:16). But in God's mercy, if we intercede, as faithful stewards, in fervent interrogative intercession for our morally plummeting society, there might come a quickening—even a dramatic move of God. We may yet see the presence and glory of Christ flooding our communities.

Will we at least try?

Prayer Points:

- Praise God as the Creator of all things and the One who determines divine purposes for every nation.
- Pray for the wisdom and enabling from God's Spirit to guard, protect, and watch over this land through your intercession.
- Ask God to use you to shape history through your prayers and obedience to His Word.
- Pray for the power of the gospel to transform hearts in ways that dramatically interrupt the decline of our society.
- Pray for the quickening of a dramatic move of God that floods your community and our nation with the glory and presence of Christ!

ACTS OF GOD IN THE NEXT GENERATION

By Luke LeFevre

I BELIEVE WE ARE HEADING into some of the greatest days of revival and spiritual awakening that our nation has ever experienced. While it may not look like how we've always assumed revival will manifest, it is coming, nonetheless. There is an undercurrent of radical, audacious faith that is filling a generation. And with faith like that, the miraculous is never far behind.

Several years ago, I spent a season in prayer. The Holy Spirit spoke to me clearly, saying, "Luke, I want you to be very careful because your generation is about to reap a harvest that it did not sow. So, stay extremely humble and give honor to those who have labored for and sown the harvest that you will reap."

I believe the unprecedented harvest we are getting ready to reap in America—and that we are already seeing—is the result of fathers and mothers who have labored, toiled, wept, and prayed for God to move. The miraculous fruit, the rare spiritual hunger, and the powerful moves of the Holy Spirit we are seeing among Gen Z are a direct result of the prayers of the generations that precede us. It is a multigenerational work.

This mixture of the prayers and labors of fathers and mothers—and the radical faith and actions of the upcoming generation—make for an explosive combination. In the days ahead, my sense is that the Lord's call to Gen Z is one of wholehearted consecration—a consecration to holy lives and to God's mission.

The great evangelist D.L. Moody once said, "The world has yet to see what God will do with a man fully consecrated to him. By God's help, I aim to be that man." I believe God is looking for just such a generation, who will say alongside D.L. Moody, "My aim is to be fully consecrated to God."

This renewed dedication to holiness and to God's mission will stir a fresh move of revival within the Church in America. And if we see revival in the Church, we can see awakening in America once again.

And if America awakens, perhaps these could be the days when the gospel reaches the very ends of the earth and the ears of all nations.

PRAYER POINTS:

- Praise God for the generations that have gone before you in prayer and faith—and how you are the recipient of those prayers.
- Pray that God will include you as the mothers and fathers of faith who have labored, wept, and prayed for a great move of God. Ask the Spirit to stir your heart to greater intercession.
- Pray for the Church to be renewed in dedication to holiness and consecration to God.
- Pray for radical, audacious faith to fill this next generation with joy and passion for Jesus.
- Pray for a fresh move of revival in the Church and spiritual awakening in this nation—so that the gospel reaches to the ends of the earth.

REVIVAL IS A CORONATION

By David Bryant

THE *MANIFEST* PRESENCE of Christ is when God reveals His Son to a new generation of His people. He does so in such dramatic fashion that it almost seems as if Christ has been hiding from us until that moment. Then suddenly He reinserts Himself among us. He *arrives*, in other words.

Revival is a "Christ-awakening movement." It is God's people waking up to God's Son for *ALL* He is, not only individually but also corporately; not only in a moment but for a season. Revival ultimately becomes a movement with wide-reaching impact on society as well as among the nations.

One could almost say that revival is like a *coronation*. In other words, it leads believers to reaffirm their wholehearted devotion to the Lamb who sits on the Throne (Rev. 5). It reconnects them to His marching orders as their King. It serves as a powerful sign of the supremacy of Christ. The renewing reality of revival should be basically defined as this: Jesus expressing Himself more fully to His people *as Lord*.

In fact, one cannot think rightly about revival at all if one does not think rightly about the glory of God's Son, Jesus Christ. He is the criterion by which we measure both revival's legitimacy and its impact. The *final revival* will emerge from fresh in-breakings of Christ's sovereign dominion before every creature in heaven and earth.

But until that final *consummation*, our Redeemer intends to continue invading His Church, extending His Lordship among us, regaining the praise He rightfully deserves, and enlarging His mission through us among all earth's peoples.

Revival is one of the most exciting expressions of Christ's supremacy that any Christian can experience until He comes again. It is prior and primary. It is the prelude to all other manifestations of Christ's reign for, in, and through His people.

Many believe a gracious "Christ Awakening" even now is bearing down on top of us, in answer to today's unprecedented global prayer movement. May it be so!

Prayer Points:

- Praise Jesus as the Lamb who sits on the throne and reigns supreme as your Lord and King!
- Pray that the manifest presence of Christ will be revealed to your generation in powerful and refreshing ways.
- Pray for a final revival that demonstrates Christ's sovereign reign before all of heaven and earth.
- Invite Jesus to invade your church with His revolutionary and transforming presence.
- Pray that the presence of Christ in your church increases the vision for gospel proclamation and mission to the world.

RISE AND SHINE

By David Bryant

R EVIVAL CAN BE DESCRIBED as when Christ "shows up" in His Church afresh to recapture us and reconquer us. Isaiah 60 suggests God's glory was *already* breaking over them like a sunrise, exposing many dimensions of His Kingdom purposes to them. What they needed to do was "rise and shine" and seize the day. These phases of revival help describe the process of waking up to Christ:

Perceive: Be aware as God's Spirit awakens believers to acknowledge not only that revival is urgently needed, but also that the promise of revival is for them.

Prioritize: Be willing to say, "A primary hope for my generation is a Christ-awakening moment, beginning in the Church. Therefore, out of my commitment to the preeminence of my Lord Jesus, I will give revival high priority in all that I do for Him."

Purify: In every revival, repentance must have precedence. Everything in us and in our congregations that disobeys the Holy Spirit—everything that is incompatible with Christ Himself, who is the focus of revival—must be confessed to the Father and put away.

Pray: Biblical and historical revivals reveal that whenever God is ready to reawaken His people to the glories of His Son, He stirs up prayer among them. Today, all of us should rejoice in the unprecedented prayer movement God has ignited among many churches and communities across our nation and world. We should do everything possible to strengthen the movement inside our own congregations.

Proclaim: Since "faith comes by hearing" (Rom. 10:17), any biblical revival must be a Word-anchored revival. Therefore, Christians should promote the biblical promises for personal and corporate revival. They also should give reports of what God has done and is doing in revival around the world.

Prepare: Though biblical revival is preeminently a corporate experience, each of us must be willing and ready to be the starting point for a fresh work of God in His Church. We should act as if we truly expect God to grant us this gracious work of His Spirit.

Partner: The hope of promised revival requires a new era of spiritual cooperation—among pastors, leaders of prayer movements, denominational leaders, and others—as we stand together to seek and to receive a God-given Christ awakening for our generation.

Rise and shine, for the glory of Christ is already breaking over us!

PRAYER POINTS:

- Praise God that "the glory of the Lord rises upon you . . . and His glory appears over you" (Isa. 60:1–2).
- Pray for God's glory to break over you, your family, and your church. Pray that it "recaptures and reconquers" you.
- Pray for an awakening to the urgent hope and promise of revival that gives preeminence to Jesus.
- Pray for the priority of repentance and urgency for holiness to characterize the Church in our nation.
- Ask God to renew a spirit of prayer and cooperation between pastors, prayer leaders, and churches of various denominations. Ask God to use your church to lead in this movement.

JESUS IN OUR MIDST

By Dave Butts

What is this thing called revival? Revival is the Church waking up to the presence of Jesus in her midst.

We believe Jesus is present when we gather as the Church. But we don't act that way. That's why your church needs revival. When church services ended last Sunday, you went home.

But what would happen if Jesus was there? Would you be looking at your watch? Would you be eager to leave? One of the characteristics of the great revivals was extended times of worship. They never wanted to end the service!

Now, obviously people had to leave because they had to take care of physical things and they had jobs that they had to go to. But as soon as they were done, they were back because that was where God was. They wanted to be in on the action. They wanted to experience God's presence.

Revival is not strange or mystical. It is simply the Church waking up to the presence of Christ in her midst. It is almost as though God reaches out and slaps us, and we wake up and realize God is there. That is what revival is. We recognize that Jesus really is here.

We are desperate for that in our nation today. I am not in any way a critic of the Church. The more I travel, the more I fall in love with the Church of Jesus Christ. I am seeing so many wonderful things happen. Christians are doing wonderful things in the name of Jesus—acts of love, mercy, and self-sacrifice. We are doing all we know to do. But it isn't working as we see the world growing increasingly dark.

In a real sense, we are at this wonderful point of despair and hopelessness. The Church is beginning to recognize that we have been doing everything we know how to do—and it is not working.

This is the time for revival. It is time to humble ourselves before God in prayer and ask Him to make Himself known in the midst of His people so that our nation can be saved and our world impacted for Christ.

PRAYER POINTS:

- Praise Jesus for His love for His Church—His Bride.
- Pray for the presence of Jesus to flood your church and awaken your congregation to the joy of revival.
- Pray for your church to wake up to Jesus as the most precious possession—and respond in a way that treasures Jesus' presence.
- Pray that our nation will recognize its desperate need for the saving and transforming presence of Jesus.
- Pray for a spiritual awakening that reveals Jesus' love for the lost—and provokes a desire to receive His salvation.

Part 5

WATCHMEN ON THE WALL

KINGDOM-FOCUSED REVIVAL PRAYER

By Dave Butts

THE ISSUE IN CHURCHES today is not that we are not praying. Every church prays some. The problem is that rarely do we pray what I call Kingdom-focused prayers.

Most of our churches are praying self-focused, need-focused prayers—our needs, our families, and things right around us. We are supposed to pray for those things, but that is only one aspect of prayer. We also should be praying every day for revival, for the completion of the task of world evangelization, for our governmental leaders, for the unsaved. Those are Kingdom-focused prayers.

In many churches, people need to move away from the common concept of revival as a week of meetings or something that we schedule. True revival is heaven-sent and is in God's hands.

A correct concept of revival helps us know what we are praying toward. Arthur Wallis wrote, "Revival is such a display of God's holiness and power that often human personalities are overshadowed and human programs abandoned. It is God breaking into the consciousness of men in majesty and glory."

The South African revivalist Andrew Murray said, "A true revival means nothing less than a revolution, casting out a spirit of worldliness and selfishness and making God in His love triumph in the heart and life."

My favorite definition is from Stephen Olford: "Revival is

ultimately Christ Himself seen, felt, heard, living, active, moving in and through His body on earth."

The whole idea of revival is a Christ-awakening. The true Church *believes* that Jesus is in their midst but is somehow failing to *experience* it. Revival crosses the great divide between our intellectual, theological, and biblical belief—and what we actually experience with Jesus' presence.

I prefer the term "revival praying" rather than "praying for revival." If I am praying *for* revival, I can become revival focused rather than focused on Christ. We want to learn to pray for what God desires to have happen—and that is the reviving presence of Jesus.

I like to think of revival praying in terms of preparing ourselves for the outpouring of the Holy Spirit. The Old Testament talks about plowing up hard or fallow ground so that if the rain falls on it, it will not just run off. The soil is drenched with life-giving water that causes everything around it to flourish.

If we prepare ourselves for the Holy Spirit to be poured out on us, we can persist in praying to God, "Give us revival! Give us revival!" Jesus will come in answer to such Kingdom-focused prayers.

PRAYER POINTS:

- Praise God for heaven-sent revival that is a true Christ-awakening. He's done it before; ask Him to do it again!
- Pray that your church goes beyond *belief* in Jesus to *experiencing* the reviving presence of Jesus.
- Pray that God prepares your church for an outpouring of the Spirit that is life-giving and causes it to flourish in your community.
- Ask God for revival that focuses on Jesus alone and manifests His Kingdom here on earth.
- Pray that God will fill you with unrelenting faith to pray, "Give us revival! Give us revival!" Pray that you do not lose hope before He does it again.

GOD'S CALL TO GUARD A NATION

By David Kubal

WHAT DOES THE future hold for the United States of America? The last few years have been full of political turmoil, civil unrest, and continued moral decline.

Israel's history during Isaiah's prophetic ministry offers us biblical lessons for our own day. The spiritual climate of Judah (the nation of Israel's Southern Kingdom) during Isaiah's early life was good. Kings Uzziah and Jotham both led Judah to follow God. As a nation, Judah remained true to Yahweh for a period, but everything changed with King Ahaz.

Ahaz committed terrible atrocities before the Lord. He defiled the temple, placed altars on street corners, and lived in open rebellion toward God. Ultimately Judah was taken captive by Nebuchadnezzar and spent 70 years in Babylonian captivity.

Isaiah's ministry took place during moral, spiritual, and cultural decline. In his early ministry (Isa. 1), the nation is accused accurately and justly, based upon the laws of God. Then Judah's idolatry is described with judicial precision (Isa. 2–5), stating the case in a manner that can only lead to one verdict: "Guilty."

Isaiah was faithful to warn Judah and prophesy God's message even though God told him his ministry would not be outwardly successful (Isa. 6:8–12). Isaiah was called to speak the truth; the people were accountable for their rejection of the message. What could be a more timely and relevant scene than this for today's intercessors?

I have found few American Christians who have a clear sense of our collective standing before God. Understanding that we have both an individual standing before God and a collective standing before God is vital to keeping a proper, honest, and God-sanctioned loyalty to both connections, giving each what is due.

Returning to the examples in Isaiah's day, the principle of all nations' accountability before God is clear. God says, "I will take vengeance in anger and wrath on the *nations that have not obeyed me*" (Micah 5:15, emphasis added).

God is justified in doing this because He is God. Romans 1 declares that all mankind has a sense of the Creator's existence and His standards. He will punish nations. It does not matter if they are ruled by dictators, kings, parliaments, or Congress.

We must be aware and accept that God holds nations accountable for their collective actions. He is justified in doing this, relying on the principle of general revelation we read about in Romans, that all of us have a sense of our Creator's desires (Rom. 1:18–23).

He will bless or hold a nation accountable based upon His laws.

PRAYER POINTS:

- Praise God that He is sovereign over all nations, and that every nation is accountable to His justice.
- Pray for God's mercy on this nation, especially as depravity increases. Pray that God will call His people collectively to fervent, humble, repentant prayer.
- Pray for the Church to recognize her role in praying fervently and using her voice to speak truth.
- Pray for the leaders of this nation. Ask God to convict them of truth and their role in honoring God's commands in His Word.

PRAYING GOD'S HEART

By Dale Schlafer

"IT WAS THE BEST OF times, it was the worst of times."

The famous opening of Charles Dickens's novel *A Tale of Two Cities* is often used to highlight a time when seemingly radical opposites coexist. Dickens continues, "It was the age of wisdom, it was the age of foolishness, it was the epoch of belief, it was the epoch of incredulity."

I thought of that line regarding what I see in the *Ecclesia* [Church] in the United States today. We are living in a time of opposites or contradictions in our communication within the Ecclesia. According to what some respected prayer leaders believe, we are moving into the greatest time the American Church has ever experienced. Revival is coming. We need to repent and pray together and then seize our destiny; we are standing on the verge of the greatest harvest in the history of the Church. This is what is coming—it is what God desires, they say.

Yet emails from other highly regarded prayer leaders contain stern warnings that the United States is moving into a time of judgment, persecution, and great hardship and that "even if Moses and Samuel stood before me pleading for these people, I wouldn't help them" (Jer. 15:1, NLT). Nothing is going to stop this judgment. It is going to occur—so get prepared.

These are radically opposite views from godly people of prayer who are, as the prophet Isaiah put it, "watchmen on [the] walls" (62:6).

What are we to believe and how are we to pray in our current seemingly contradictory situation?

We are not spinning out of control to some unknown end. God is the Watchman over history, sovereignly directing the best and worst of times. The question for people of prayer is, *are we listening to God or merely praying what we want?*

Peter gives the entire Ecclesia the responsibility of being alert watchmen: "The end of all things is near. Therefore be alert and of sober mind so that you may pray" (1 Peter 4:7).

We are to observe what is transpiring around us and go to God to learn how to pray. The entire body of Christ has the responsibility to watch, and if you will, to act as watchmen.

PRAYER POINTS:

- Praise God that He is the Watchman over all history—and nothing is out of His control!
- Ask God to increase your sensitivity to the Spirit as you watch and pray God's heart.
- Pray for humility in recognizing the different perspectives in the body of Christ—and that only God knows all things. Pray for blessing upon those believers who may differ from your views.
- Pray that the Church will be alert and of sober mind in prayer about "the end of all things."
- Invite God to establish you as a watchman in your intercession, that you will pray His heart and trust Him in strategic times.

WATCH AND PRAY

By Jacquie Tyre

IN MY JOURNEY as a watchman, the most important aspect has been what I will call the "Habakkuk 2 Watch." Habakkuk 2 starts out with the prophet declaring his posture and intent:

> I will stand at my watch and station myself on the ramparts;
>
> I will look to see what He will say to me.

It is important to remember that Habakkuk is in a faith struggle. The people of Israel are facing challenges at the hands of the Chaldeans, and Habakkuk is wrestling with the way things are going for the people of God. In his wrestling, he turns to seek the Lord, to "watch to see what He will say."

In all our watching, no matter what the situation, we begin and end with seeking to know what God is doing—or what He desires to do. Jesus instructed His disciples to "Seek first his kingdom and his righteousness" (Matt. 6:33). Seeking the Lord first will protect us against all manner of distraction, discouragement, and deception.

So how do we watch? We watch by seeking the Lord's face (2 Chron. 7:14; Ps. 27:8; Hos. 5:15), by meditating upon the Word of God (Josh. 1:8; Ps. 1:2, 63:6), by listening for His voice (Deut. 32:1–3; Ps. 95:6–8; John 10:3), and by observing the things around us with eyes of faith (Deut. 28–30; 1 Chron. 12:32; 2 Chron. 6; Mark 4:26–29).

When we have discovered what He is doing, then, as Henry Black-aby says in *Experiencing God,* we simply join Him in what He is doing. As we join the Lord in prayer, we enter into a place of agreement with the will of heaven. Our prayers rise with faith-filled confidence toward His will being done on earth as it is in heaven according to the Lord's model prayer (Matt. 6:9–13).

Today, as we look at the circumstances of the world around us, it can become annoying, overwhelming, and even terrifying at times. However, the Lord makes His grace available to us to watch with eyes of faith and pray for discernment to know how to respond in His wisdom and power.

PRAYER POINTS:

- Praise God that He rules over nations and is engaged with His people. He has plans that will not be thwarted.
- Pray for eyes to see His purposes for our nation and the world—and how you can join Him in what He's already doing.
- Ask God to give you faith-filled confidence in your prayers as you agree with His will in both heaven and on earth.
- Ask God to pour out His grace and inspire your prayers in confusing and terrifying times.
- Pray for eyes of faith and hearts of discernment that align your prayers perfectly with God's plans.

DISCERNING THE TIMES

By Bill Elliff

A LEADER IS ONE WHO has the foresight to see where a family, an organization, a business, a church, or a movement is going. Discerning leaders anticipate the coming waves—and know how to take people through them.

For followers of Christ, such spiritual leadership is invaluable. Scan your Bible. You will see that the men or women who were used by God to change the world around them, also had the ability to see ahead. They understood the times.

Discerning prophets warned people, and their warnings, if heeded, saved whole nations. Joseph had dreams that delivered the known world, including his own family. David stayed one step ahead of a murderous Saul. Elijah saw "horses and chariots of fire," a heavenly sighting that brought peace to his servant and deliverance to his people (2 Kings 6:15–17).

Discernment is indispensable for prayer. Effective intercessors, in tune with God's understanding, don't waste their prayers. They get in the loop of Spirit-initiated intercession in such ways that their prayers help God's "kingdom come and will be done on earth, as it is in heaven" (Matt. 6:10).

How can you discern the times? *Read your Bible!* Read it thoroughly, prayerfully, daily—and seek to know the ways of God and man. Then interpret everything that is happening around you in light of God's ways.

Do you know what is happening in our nation right now? Are you praying rightly? God has given you what you need in His Word to be like the men of Issachar who "understood the times" and "knew what Israel should do" (1 Chron. 12:32). God's Word is not given merely to help you devotionally, but to equip you for insightful, discerning intercession that moves heaven and earth!

This type of prayer starts in the heavens, passes through the discerning intercessor, and returns to the Throne. Such prayer is effective because it is initiated by God Himself. God loves to answer His own desires.

We are entering days that we have never seen in our lifetime. Evil days. Critical days. This calls for a new level of intercession. We need men and women who see ahead and pray fervently, faithfully, and effectively.

God is not unaware of these days. He has been navigating His Church, with all our weaknesses, through the darkness of this world for decades. The gates of hell will never prevail against His agenda. He can make you an intercessor who sees ahead and helps heaven and earth move for His glory.

PRAYER POINTS:

- Praise God for His Word that equips us with discernment and an understanding of the times.
- Pray for spiritual leadership in your church to grow deeper in their prayer and understanding of God's purposes.
- Pray that God will inspire you with Spirit-led intercession that brings His Kingdom here on earth.
- Pray that you and your church will engage in a new level of intercession that rightly reflects God's heart for a lost and dark world.
- Pray for the discernment you need to pray faith-filled prayers that move heaven and earth for God's glory.

Part 6

END TIMES
URGENCY

THE LORD IS NEAR

By Bob Bakke

U NLESS YOU'RE LIVING under a rock or in a monastic retreat, you can't escape the storm clouds gathering on the horizon of history. Storms always loom somewhere, but particularly ill winds are blowing today—and we can hear alarms sounding from every direction. Tensions are rising in every society.

In the United States various ideologies are clashing over who's to blame for the present difficulties and the best direction for the future of America.

Anxious Americans are seeing gun sales soaring. Violent religious and philosophical hatreds play out on the evening news. Meanwhile, jihadist groups are scouring the world for weapons of mass destruction—chemical or nuclear—to employ against Western interests.

Those who remain faithful to Christ feel as though their faith is under assault from entertainers, government officials, journalists, coworkers, classmates, teachers, neighbors, and family members. Powerful voices are labeling biblical Christianity as a hate crime. Freedom of speech is eroding.

But to be honest, the earth has witnessed periods like this before. Thirty years ago, nuclear-armed communism compelled us to think the end imminent. Seventy years ago, the axis of Nazi Germany and Imperial Japan threatened the world.

It's safe to say that God expects Christians in every generation to watch carefully for the signs of Jesus' return and to ask whether their generation will see the heavens open and Jesus descend. Even though we've been wrong about Jesus' return in the past, God has still graciously answered our prayers for His greater glory.

In each of the above periods, God sent revivals, even though it wasn't yet the new age to come. My friend David Bryant calls these revivals "approximations of the consummation." In other words, as we are stirred to prayer because of the events of our day, God answers by giving us a taste of what the return of Jesus will be like.

But God also answers our prayers because both the Bible and history give explicit evidence that God stands ready to pour out His Spirit in troubled times if His people pursue Him in holiness. Whether Jesus comes in the next 24 hours or 24 months, or in the 24th century, one thing is crystal clear: *What is happening today should compel us to be fully awake and carefully watching for signs of His coming.*

In this there is no doubt. The Church and the nations of the earth need an out-pouring of the Holy Spirit that foreshadows the Lordship of Christ over all things.

PRAYER POINTS:

- Invite the Lord to open your eyes to clearly see the storm clouds gathered on the horizon of this nation. Ask God for His perspective as to how you might pray urgently for both revival and Jesus' soon return.

- Praise God for the historical and biblical examples of God's willingness to pour out His Spirit in answer to the prayers of His people. Ask Him to do it again in our day.

- Pray for a stirring of holiness in God's people and a willingness to pursue Him for revival.

- Pray that your church will be fully awake and carefully watching for the next great move of God.

MORNING AND NIGHT ARE COMING

By Dale Schlafer

SCRIPTURE SAYS, "If the trumpet does not sound a *clear* call, who will get ready for battle?" (1 Cor. 14:8, emphasis added). But respected watchmen on the walls today appear to be giving two conflicting messages. As a result, there is great confusion in the Ecclesia [Church].

One group of watchmen says we are moving into the greatest days in the history of the American Church. The other says we are facing God's imminent judgment and very difficult days.

Having wrestled with this, I'm proposing something I believe the Lord has helped me grasp. In Isaiah 21:11–12 we read: "'Watchman, what is left of the night? Watchman, what is left of the night?' The watchman replies, 'Morning is coming, but also the night.'" It sounds as though the watchman doesn't understand.

But perhaps we are the ones who are confused. The morning is coming. There is going to be a great harvest of lost souls, spectacular displays of God's glory, and great healings to observe. At the same time, the watchman says, "Also the night."

I see that a time of great difficulty and hardship is also coming. The United States will go through great judgment that no amount of repentance, fasting, and prayer can restrain.

Could it be that the Lord wants us to recognize that when we see

81

only one of the messages, we are receiving only part of what watchmen are to see? Could it be that God is saying we need both mindsets as we move closer to Christ's return?

If this is true, then it changes how we pray. What if, biblically, we are to expect a mighty move of God in the midst of great darkness and judgment? What if we are indeed moving into a time of deep darkness but in the midst of it the light of Christ will shine more brightly?

God is the Watchman over it all, so let's keep praying according to His heart. "Watchman, what is left of the night? Watchman, what is left of the night?"

The watchman replies, "Morning is coming, but also the night."

PRAYER POINTS:

- Praise God that He rules over both the morning and the night, light and darkness. Express your trust in Him no matter what comes your way.
- Pray with an expectant heart for a great move of God and an unprecedented harvest of lost people.
- Ask God to prepare you to be the light of Christ to others, even if it is in the midst of persecution and hardship.
- Pray that you will be an alert and discerning watchman on the wall as you pray toward the Lord's return.
- Pray that even in darkness, the Church will be the brilliant light of the glory of Christ to our nation and the world.

Day 30

HEAVEN WAITS FOR OUR PRAYERS

By Bob Bakke

IN THE 1740s, Jonathan Edwards preached a series of sermons on the millennial reign of Christ. Out of this series came not only an influential book, but the launch of The Concert of Prayer—a prayer movement that became the common denominator to hundreds of revivals, three international awakenings, and the explosion of international missions.

In one of the key passages, Edwards addresses Revelation 8, in which the Lamb of God takes the scroll from His Father and opens the seven seals—that is, when God inaugurates the consummation of history. Instead of an explosion of activity, however, we read the following: "When he opened the seventh seal, there was silence in heaven for about half an hour" (v. 1).

Everything in heaven stopped. In silence heaven waited.

But why did heaven wait? We soon learn this:

> Another angel, who had a golden censer, came and stood at the altar. He was given much incense to offer, *with the prayers of all the saints*, on the golden altar before the throne. The smoke of the incense, together with the prayers of the saints, went up before God from the angel's hand. Then the angel took the censer, filled it with fire from the altar, and hurled it on the earth; and there came peals of thunder, rumblings, flashes of lightning

and an earthquake (vv. 3–5, emphasis added).

In other words, when it came to the end of all things and the return of Christ, heaven waited for "the prayers of all the saints." Upon the evidence of Revelation 8, Edwards was convinced the second coming of Christ would be preceded by a great and global movement of prayer. In private, he speculated that it would be sometime soon after the year 2000.

Could he be right about the date? Today there is an unprecedented movement of united prayer across the earth. Was he right about the power of united prayer with regard to the purposes of Christ? Absolutely.

As with revivals of the past—and the great missionary and church-planting movements that emerged from them—God may want to accomplish many great things before the coming of His Son. Even today we are witnessing great harvests of souls—the largest in the history of the Church. This age of the Holy Spirit is yielding remarkable fruit.

May the certainty of Jesus' return keep us on our knees. Our generation will thank us for our prayers.

PRAYER POINTS:

- Praise God that we can rest in the assurance of the return of Christ in God's perfect timing.
- Pray that God will pour out His Spirit and accomplish great things for His Kingdom before Jesus' return.
- Pray for a growing crescendo of the prayers of the saints to fill the throne room of heaven and inaugurate the consummation of history.
- Pray for church-planting movements to explode and a great harvest of souls to precede His coming.
- Ask God to raise up His Church in the greatest global movement of prayer in the history of the world!

THE NATIONAL PRAYER ACCORD

THE NATIONAL PRAYER ACCORD is patterned after a rhythm of prayer established by Jonathan Edwards and churches in the colonies prior to the First Great Awakening in the United States. In more recent days, many prayer and revival ministries are encouraging believers and churches to adopt this ongoing rhythm of prayer in their own circles.

In Recognition of:
- Our absolute dependence on God
- The moral and spiritual challenges facing our nation
- Our national need for repentance and divine intervention
- The covenants of prayer that God has answered throughout history
- Our great hope for a general awakening to the lordship of Christ, the unity of His Body, and the sovereignty of His Kingdom

We strongly urge all churches and followers of Jesus in America to unite in seeking the face of God through prayer and fasting, persistently asking our Father to send revival to the Church and spiritual awakening to our nation so that Christ's Great Commission might be fulfilled worldwide in our generation.

This voluntary agreement in prayer seems "good to the Holy Spirit and to us" (Acts 15:28) in light of the promise of Jesus in Matthew 18:19 and the unity for which Jesus prayed in John 17. This prayer accord presupposes a spirit of freedom to adjust its component parts as local Christians see need.

Though many are seeking God more often than this prayer accord outlines, calling millions of others around focused times of prayer is an urgent need.

We resolve to promote as an ongoing "Rhythm of Prayer" . . .

Weekly . . . In private or small group prayer, which lends itself to a focus on the regular preaching and teaching of God's Word, asking the Holy Spirit to light the fires of revival by anointing our preachers and teachers each week.

Monthly . . . In local ministry prayer gatherings, such as a mid-week prayer meeting, a Bible study class, a Sunday evening service, a home group, or one meeting of a college campus group, etc. for the exclusive purpose of prayer for revival.

Quarterly . . . In prayer gatherings among local ministries and groups, uniting churches in a community, college ministries in the area, businessmen's groups, or radio listeners for an evening meeting, a luncheon, or a segment of airtime focusing on prayer for the community or region.

Annually . . . In prayer meetings designed to unite Christians nationally, such as the National Day of Prayer, the first Thursday of May, and Cry Out America, September 11 each year—occasions that call millions of people to pray together.

The National Prayer Committee and its partners offer tools, templates, and stories to help facilitate this prayer accord (nationalprayeraccord.com), while recommending that other ministries do the same.

Downstream in America we find the symptoms and signs of church irrelevance, fragmented relationships, cultural decay, moral decline, and love growing cold, but Upstream from such symptoms, we find hope in united prevailing prayer.

- "… but I have prayed for you and when you are restored strengthen others" (Luke 22:32). As certainly as Jesus prayed for Peter, He prays for us!
- "Jesus Christ is the same yesterday and today, yes forever" (Hebrews 13:8).
- "He always lives to make intercession" (Hebrews 7:25).
- "Christ Jesus is He … who also intercedes for us" (Romans 8:33).

We resolve to promote as "Prayer Goals" the outpouring of God's Spirit for …

The Revival of the Church as Evidenced by the Indicators of Awakening in the Church:

1. Increasing testimony of the manifest presence of God.
2. Increased conversions and baptisms.
3. Amplified participation in corporate as well as individual prayer, fasting, and other spiritual disciplines leading to more effective discipleship.
4. A decrease in divorces and renewed commitment to marriage between a man and a woman in covenant relationship as God intends.
5. Imparting faith to children and youth as parents are equipped by the church to become primary disciplers of their children.
6. Among churches, a passionate pursuit for the well-being of their cities through the planting of new congregations, benevo-

lent ministries, practical service, and focused evangelism.

7. Commitment to radical generosity as evidenced by compassion ministries and global missions.

8. Improved health among ministers as evidenced by their joy, decreased resignations, healthy loving relationships within their families, and an increased response among young people called to the ministry.

9. Christians involved in bold witness accompanied by miracles, dramatic conversions, and Holy Spirit empowered victories over evil.

10. Heightened expressions of love and unity among all believers, as demonstrated by the unity of pastors and leaders.

The Advancement of the Kingdom as Evidenced by These Indicators of Awakening in the Culture:

1. Breakdowns of racial, social, and status barriers as Christ's church celebrates together—Jesus!

2. A restoration of morality, ethical foundations and accountability among leaders of church and government, business and politics.

3. A transformation of society through the restoration of Christ's influence in the arts, media, and communications.

4. Increased care for the hungry and homeless, the most vulnerable and needy.

5. Young adults, students, and children embracing the claims and lifestyle of Christ through the witness of peers who live and love as Jesus.

6. Community and national leaders seeking out the church as an answer to society's problems.

7. Increased care for children as "gifts from the Lord" as the gospel

addresses abortion, adoption, foster care, and child well-being.

8. Righteous relations between men and women: decrease in divorce rates, cohabitation, same-sex relations, sexual abuse, sexual trafficking, out-of-wedlock children, and STDs.

9. An awakening to the "fear of the Lord" rather than the approval of people, thus restoring integrity and credibility.

10. Neighborhood transformation and an accompanying decrease of social ills through increased expressions of "loving your neighbor" in service, compassion, and unity.

Developed by America's National Prayer Committee in partnership with One-Cry and the Awakening America Alliance.

SOURCES OF CONTENT

2012.

18. Longing for Change: David Kubal, Issue 22, September–October 2015.

19. The Acts of God in the Next Generation: Luke LeFevre, Issue 47, January–March 2022.

20. Revival Is a Coronation: David Bryant, Issue 2, January–February 2012.

21. Rise and Shine: David Bryant, Issue 2, January–February 2012.

22. *When God Shows Up:* Dave Butts, PrayerShop Publishing, 2013.

23. *When God Shows Up:* Dave Butts, PrayerShop Publishing, 2013.

24. God's Call to Guard a Nation: David Kubal, Issue 28, January–March 2017.

25. Praying God's Heart: Dale Schlafer, Issue 28, January–March 2017.

26. Watch and Pray: Jacquie Tyre, Issue 8; January–February 2013.

27. Discerning the Times: Bill Elliff, April–June 2017, Issue 29.

28. The Lord Is Near: Bob Bakke, Issue 8, January–February 2013.

29. Morning and Night Are Coming: Dale Schlafer, Issue 28, January–March 2017.

30. Heaven Waits for Our Prayers: Bob Bakke, Issue 8, January–February 2013.

ABOUT THE EDITOR AND CONTRIBUTORS

Carol Madison is editor of *Prayer Connect* magazine, author of *Prayer That's Caught and Taught*, and director of prayer ministries at Hillside Church of Bloomington, MN.

About the Contributors

Bob Bakke is on the executive leadership team of OneCry.

Dan and Melissa Jarvis serve on the leadership team of Life Action Ministries.

Jim Jarman is an intercultural church planter in Stockholm, Sweden.

David Kubal is CEO and president of Intercessors for America.

Doug Small is president and founder of Alive Ministries: Project Pray.

Byron Paulus is on the executive leadership team of OneCry.

Bill Elliff is on the executive leadership team of OneCry.

Kay Horner is executive director of Awakening America Alliance.

Dave Butts was president of Harvest Prayer Ministries, chairman of America's National Prayer Committee, and a member of OneCry's executive leadership team.

David Bryant directs Project Hope and is former chairman of America's National Prayer Committee.

Luke LeFevre is the visionary and director of Consecrated.

Dale Schlafer is president and cofounder of the Center for World Revival and Awakening.

Jacquie Tyre is president and founder of Kairos Transformation Ministries.

*Prayer*CONNECT

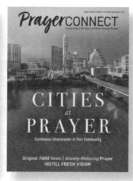

A QUARTERLY MAGAZINE DESIGNED TO:

Mobilize believers to pray God's purposes for their church, city and nation.

Connect intercessors with the growing worldwide prayer movement.

Equip prayer leaders and pastors with tools to disciple their congregations.

EACH ISSUE OF PRAYER CONNECT INCLUDES:

- Practical articles to equip and inspire your prayer life.
- Helpful prayer tips and proven ideas.
- News of prayer movements around the world.
- Theme articles exploring important prayer topics.
- Connections to prayer resources available online

Print subscription: $29.99 (includes digital version)
Digital subscription: $23.99
Church Prayer Leaders Network membership: $49.99
(includes print, digital, and CPLN membership benefits)

SUBSCRIBE NOW.
www.prayerleader.com/membership or call 812-238-5504